AF270355

Proteins as Necessary Nutrients

BY AMY C. REA

Kids Core
An Imprint of Abdo Publishing
abdobooks.com

abdobooks.com

Published by Abdo Publishing, a division of ABDO, PO Box 398166, Minneapolis, Minnesota 55439. Copyright © 2023 by Abdo Consulting Group, Inc. International copyrights reserved in all countries. No part of this book may be reproduced in any form without written permission from the publisher. Kids Core™ is a trademark and logo of Abdo Publishing.

Printed in the United States of America, North Mankato, Minnesota.
102022
012023

Cover Photo: Mara Ze/Shutterstock Images
Interior Photos: Shutterstock Images, 4–5, 8, 10–11, 14 (top row), 14 (bottom left), 14 (bottom center), 14 (bottom right), 28 (top), 28 (bottom), 29 (bottom); iStockphoto, 6, 12, 13; Steve Gschmeissner/Science Source, 16; Tatiana Bralnina/Shutterstock Images, 18–19; Elena Eryomenko/Shutterstock Images, 21; Prostock Studio/iStockphoto, 23; Julia Sudnitskaya/Shutterstock Images, 25; Mara Ze/Shutterstock Images, 26; Julia Yelfimova/Shutterstock Images, 29 (top)

Editor: Amanda Lanser
Series Designer: Layna Darling

Library of Congress Control Number: 2022940686

Publisher's Cataloging-in-Publication Data

Names: Rea, Amy C., author.
Title: Proteins as necessary nutrients / by Amy C. Rea
Description: Minneapolis, Minnesota: Abdo Publishing, 2023 | Series: Necessary nutrients | Includes online resources and index.
Identifiers: ISBN 9781098290047 (lib. bdg.) | ISBN 9781098275242 (ebook)
Subjects: LCSH: Proteins--Juvenile literature. | Food--Protein content--Juvenile literature. | Proteins in human nutrition--Juvenile literature. | Nutrition--Health aspects--Juvenile literature.
Classification: DDC 613.2--dc23

CONTENTS

Proteins help hair grow.

CHAPTER 1

Proteins

Elle wanted to grow her hair all the way down to her waist. It was only at her shoulders. It seemed like her hair was growing too slowly. Elle complained to her mom, who was a nurse.

Proteins help build muscles and bones.

Elle's mom told her how to fix the problem. She could eat foods to help her hair grow. Elle was surprised. She did not know food could affect her hair. Her mother said some foods contain proteins. Proteins are in hair. They help hair grow. That afternoon, Elle had a handful of almonds for a snack. Almonds had more protein than her usual crackers. Elle couldn't wait for her hair to start growing faster!

Protein in the Body

Proteins are not just in hair. The body uses proteins in many different ways. They are in muscles, bones, and skin. Proteins are in nearly all body parts and **tissues**.

Proteins are made of amino acids. Amino acids are protein building blocks. They combine to create the shapes of proteins.

Eat Proteins Daily

The body can store some **nutrients** to use later. However, it cannot store proteins. People must eat foods with proteins every day. It is best to get some protein with every meal. That gives the body protein throughout the day. Some snacks, such as cheese and nuts, have proteins.

People get macronutrients from the foods they eat.

Twenty kinds of amino acids make up proteins. The body makes some of these amino acids. It must get others from food.

Humans need many kinds of **nutrients**. Nutrients are substances in food. They help bodies grow and stay healthy. The body needs three types of nutrients most. They are proteins, fats, and carbohydrates. These are called macronutrients. Macronutrients give the body energy. They help it stay healthy.

Further Evidence

Look at the website below. Does it give any new information about proteins that was not in Chapter One?

Protein

abdocorelibrary.com/proteins-as
-necessary-nutrients

Proteins support a
child's growth.

CHAPTER 2

Why the Body Needs Proteins

Proteins are the body's building blocks. The body is made up of trillions of structures called **cells**. Cells turn nutrients into energy. They give the body its structure. Cells need protein to work well. Proteins help the body repair cells and make new ones.

Proteins keep the body healthy and help people play sports.

They help people grow, stay healthy, and become strong. Eating enough protein is important for adults and for children.

Some proteins build muscles. They help the body be active without becoming tired.

Proteins help build strong bones in children and adults.

They keep the body at a healthy weight. Proteins can strengthen bones. Strong bones help the body move properly. They give the body structure. Eating proteins throughout a person's life helps bones stay strong.

Other proteins move nutrients through the body in the blood. These proteins carry nutrients into and out of the body's cells. Every part of the body gets the nutrients it needs.

What Proteins Do

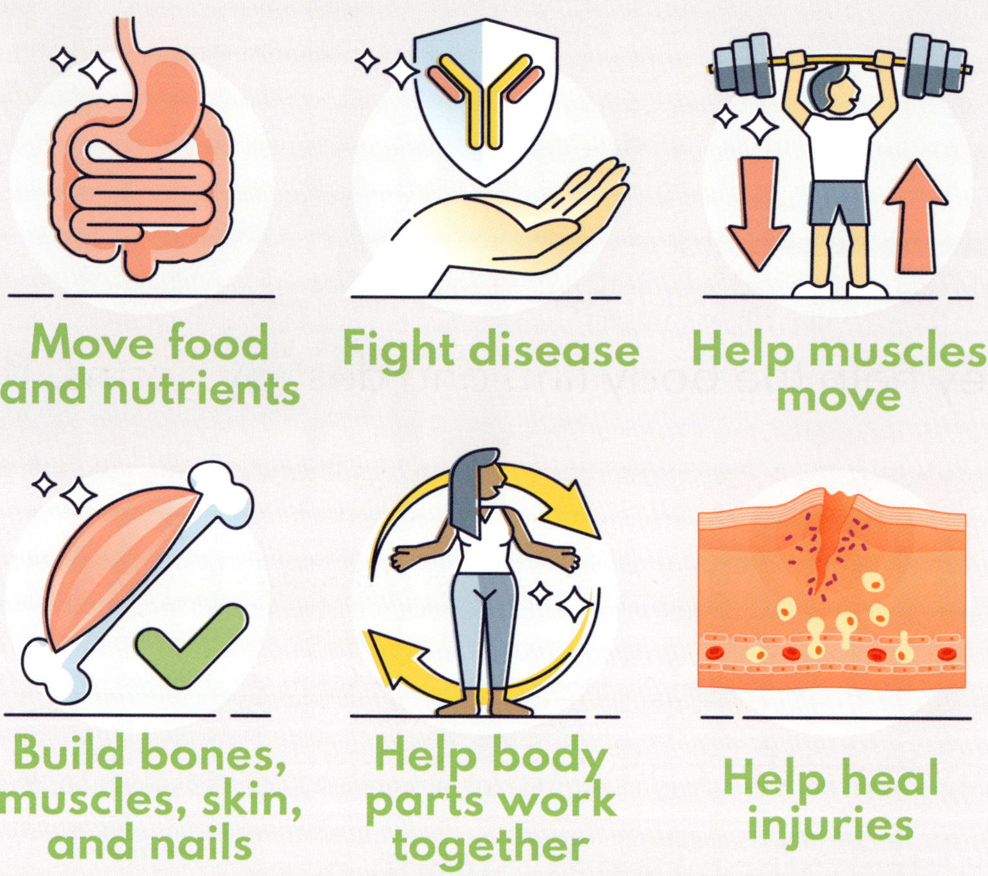

Proteins do important work within the body.

Eating snacks and meals with protein helps the body feel full longer. That helps keep body weight at a healthy level.

Protecting and Healing the Body

Some proteins fight germs and **infections**. They help the body find and destroy germs. This protects the body from illness. Proteins also help heal injuries. They reduce swelling around the injury. They create new tissue at the site of the injury.

What the Body Needs

The food a person eats provides energy from **calories**. Between 10 and 35 percent of a person's daily calories should come from protein. Exactly how much protein someone needs varies. Younger people need more protein to grow. Active people also need more protein to build and repair muscle.

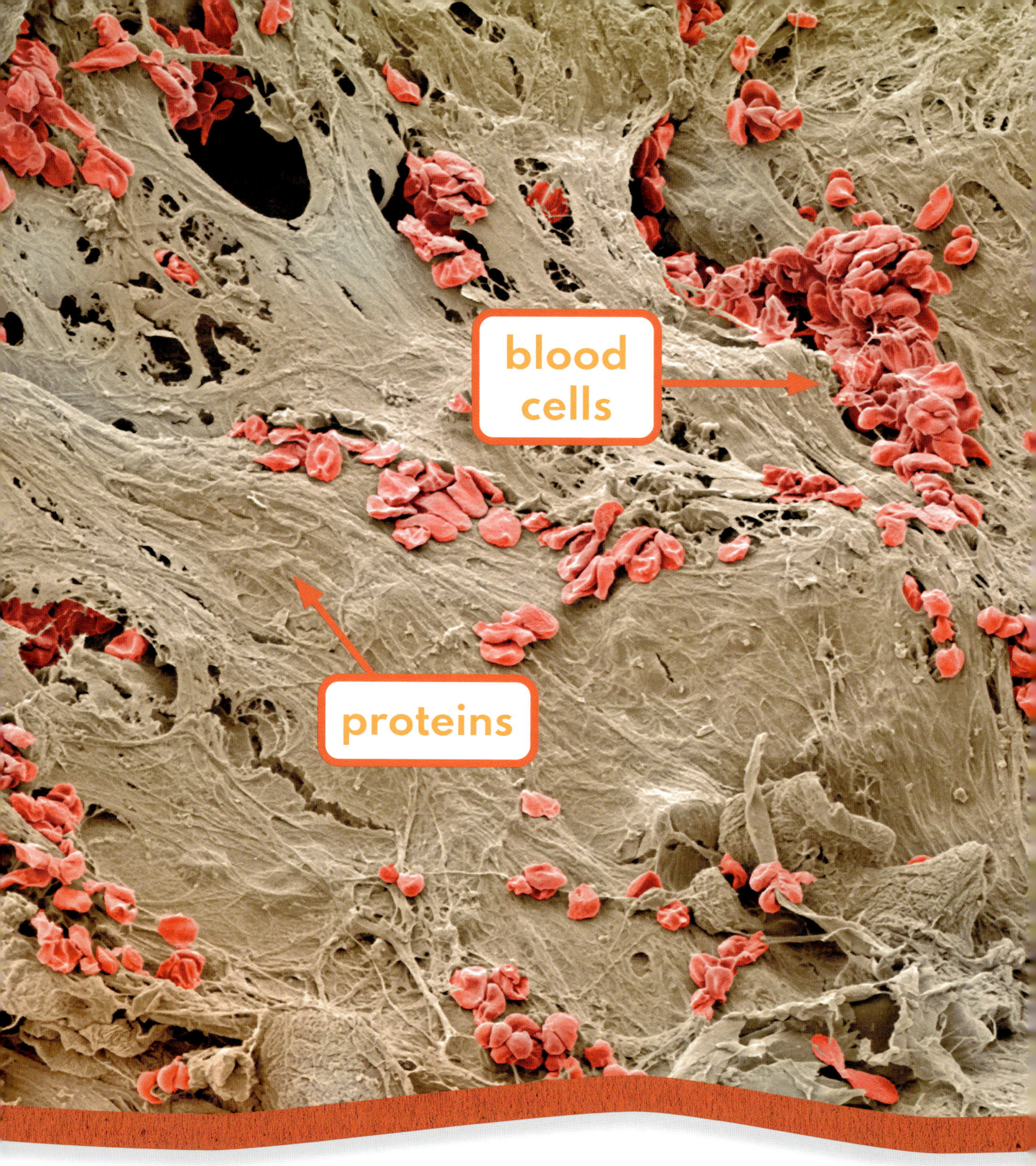

Proteins help the body heal scrapes, cuts, and other injuries.

Proteins are important for every part of the body. They support the function of many of the body's systems. Proteins are the building blocks of good health.

Explore Online

Visit the website below. Does it give any new information about how protein works in the body?

Why Is Protein Important in Your Diet?

abdocorelibrary.com/proteins-as -necessary-nutrients

Meats can be healthy sources of protein.

CHAPTER 3

Foods That Provide Protein

People need to eat foods with protein every day. Many foods provide protein. But not all of them are healthy choices.

Protein can be found in foods from animals and plants. Dairy products, including yogurt and cheese, are made from milk.

These foods contain proteins. So does the meat from animals, such as chicken, beef, and fish. Skinless chicken, fish, eggs, and low-fat dairy products are healthy protein choices. Some foods with protein include other nutrients too. Salmon is high in protein. It also contains healthy fats called omega-3 **fatty acids**. Omega-3 fatty acids are good for the body, especially the heart.

Eating Insects

Insects are eaten in many parts of Asia, South America, and Africa. It can be difficult to raise animals in these areas. Insects are easier to raise. They need less land and food. They are important sources of protein.

Salmon has protein and healthy omega-3 fatty acids.

Making Healthy Choices

Dairy and meat products can be healthy sources of protein. But some of these foods contain unhealthy substances. Dairy and meat may contain saturated fat. This type of fat is solid at room temperature. It can cause heart disease. It can cause other health issues. Processed meats such as hot dogs and bacon are high in saturated fats. They also have less protein than other types of meat.

Plants Provide Protein Too

Foods from animals are good sources of protein. But people can get enough protein just from eating plants. Beans, peas, soybeans, peanuts, and lentils are good protein sources.

Milk and other dairy products are good sources of protein.

So are nuts and seeds. Whole-grain foods such as oats, spelt, and amaranth contain protein. Some vegetables, such as corn and broccoli, provide protein too.

Getting Enough Protein

The amount of protein people need varies. Age, weight, and physical activity make a difference in how much protein a person needs.

Most adults need about 0.25 ounces (7 g) of protein per 20 pounds (9 kg) of body weight. Children ages four to nine need 0.67 ounces (19 g) of protein every day. Eating foods with protein at every meal provides what most people need.

Nuts, seeds, and some other plant foods have a lot of protein.

Three eggs contain the amount of protein children four to nine years old need each day.

Proteins do many things to help the body. Eating healthy sources of protein gives the body some of the nutrients it needs.

Doctors at the Cleveland Clinic, a US medical center, described children's protein needs:

> Children should get enough protein every day for basic needs and athletics if they eat two servings of lean protein. . . . Anything additional . . . likely exceeds their daily needs.

Source: "Why Extra Protein for Your Child Is Unnecessary and Possibly Dangerous." *Cleveland Clinic: Health Essentials*, 10 Aug. 2021, health.clevelandclinic.org. Accessed 27 Apr. 2022.

Comparing Texts

Think about the quote. Does it support the information in this chapter? Or does it give a different perspective? Explain how in two to three sentences.

Nutrient Jobs

Proteins help
the body grow.

Proteins help the
body fight infection.

Proteins help
muscles move.

Proteins help
injuries heal faster.

Glossary

calories
units for measuring the amount of energy food makes when eaten

cells
the smallest and most basic units of life

fatty acids
the building blocks of fat

infections
illnesses caused by germs

nutrients
substances needed for the body's health

tissue
a group of cells that have a similar structure and act together to perform specific functions

Online Resources

To learn more about proteins as necessary nutrients, visit our free resource websites below.

Visit **abdocorelibrary.com** or scan this QR code for free Common Core resources for teachers and students, including vetted activities, multimedia, and booklinks, or deeper subject comprehension.

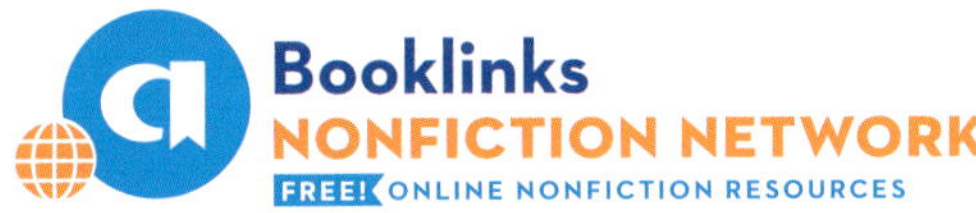

Visit **abdobooklinks.com** or scan this QR code for free additional online weblinks for further learning. These links are routinely monitored and updated to provide the most current information available.

Learn More

Golkar, Golriz. *The Immune System*. Abdo, 2023.

Troup, Roxanne. *The Circulatory System*. Abdo, 2023.

Ziemann, Kimberly. *Fats as Necessary Nutrients*. Abdo, 2023.

Index

About the Author

Amy C. Rea grew up in northern Minnesota and now lives in a Minneapolis suburb with her family. She writes frequently about traveling around Minnesota and loves to spend time with her dog.